DEAR,

May the Almighty bless you and your family with his blessing.

Angels & Jinn; Who are they?
A brief explanation for Muslim kids about Invisible & Supernatural beings created by Allah Al-Mighty

ISBN: 978-1-990544-94-1

CREATURES OF ALLAH(S.W.T) IN THE UNIVERSE

In Islam, Muslims believe in the existence of all of the creatures that Allah(S.W.T) has created, which other than humankind and animal kingdom, includes Jinn and Angels. Both Jinn and Angels exist parallel to human beings, and there are interactions between them. However, we cannot see them; thus, they are referred to as "unseen creatures". From Islam's two authentic sources of evidence, the Qur'an and Hadith (recorded deeds and sayings of Prophet Muhammad ﷺ), we have true information about the history and characteristics of these beings.

ANGELS

NATURE & APPEARANCE

Angels, 'malaikah' in Arabic, are a creation of Allah(S.W.T) and are made of "Noor (light)". They were created before mankind, always following the commands of Allah(S.W.T). Allah Al-Mighty is in no need of these creatures, but having knowledge and belief in them adds to the awe that one feels towards God; for indeed the magnificence of His creation is a proof of the magnificence of the Creator. Angels are obedient creatures by nature as they do not deviate from obeying God's directives; they do not have a free will, and therefore they are free of all sins. There is no concept of 'fallen angels' in Islam as they never disobey Allah's order. They are neither God's associates running different districts of the universe nor objects to be worshipped or prayed to. They all submit to Allah(S.W.T) and carry out His commands in both the invisible and the physical world. They also don't have families and do not need to sleep, eat or drink.

The Qur'an says:

"And to Allah ˹alone˺ bows down ˹in submission˺ whatever is in the heavens and whatever is on the earth of living creatures, as do the angels— and they (are) not arrogant." (Surah An-Nahl, V:49)

"Who (angels) never disobey whatever Allah orders—always doing as commanded."
(Surah At-Tahrim, V:6)

Angels love the believers and doers of good deeds and beseech Allah to forgive them their sins. They do not get bored or tired of worshipping Allah(S.W.T):

"They celebrate His praises night and day, nor do they ever slacken." (Suran Al-Anbya, V:20)

Qur'an and Hadiths tell us about several facts and the unique appearance of the angels. They have acted as a messenger of the God and communicated with the several Prophets of Allah in human form.

"All praise is for Allah, the Originator of the heavens and the earth, Who made angels ˹as His˺ messengers with wings—two, three, or four. He increases in creation whatever He wills. Surely Allah is Most Capable of everything."
(Surah Fatir 35:1)

Some of their characteristics are:

- They are neither male nor female.

- They can take on the form of humans.

- They have wings, sometimes in pairs of two, three or four.

- They are extremely beautiful except for the Angel of Death.

Only God knows the total amount of Angels in the universe; seven skies and earth combined. But according to some Hadiths, we can estimate that there are many angels assigned with specific duties by Allah(S.W.T). In a hadith about Miraj; the night journey, and the ascension to the Heavens of the Messenger of Allah ﷺ, The Holy Prophet ﷺ said:

"Then, I was shown Al-Bait-al-Ma'mur (i.e. Allah's House). I asked Jibrael(A.S) about it, and he said, "This is Al Bait-ul-Ma'mur where 70,000 angels perform prayers daily, and when they leave they never return to it (but always a fresh batch comes into it daily)" (Sahih Bukhari 3207; Sahih Muslim 164)

"˜Remember, O Prophet,˜ when you said to the believers, "Is it not enough that your Lord will send down a reinforcement of three thousand angels for your aid?"
(Surah Al-Imran, 124)

THE SIGNIFICANCE OF BELIEF IN ANGELS IN ISLAM

"The Messenger ˋfirmlyˋ believes in what has been revealed to him from his Lord, and so do the believers. They ˋallˋ believe in Allah, His angels, His Books, and His messengers. ˋThey proclaim,ˋ "We make no distinction between any of His messengers." And they say, "We hear and obey. ˋWe seekˋ Your forgiveness, our Lord! And to You ˋaloneˋ is the final return."
(Surah Al-Baqarah 2:285)

The Six Beliefs of Islam are the fundamental beliefs that every Muslim holds to be true. Among these six, the belief in angels, as mentioned in the Qur'an and the authentic Hadiths of the Holy Prophet ﷺ, is an indispensable part necessary for the completion of the Muslim faith. In Islam, the six believes of faith are as follows:

- *Tawhid* - Belief in the oneness of Allah

- *Malaika* - Belief in the existence of angels of Allah

- Belief in the *Holy books* of Allah; Zabur, Torah, Gospel, and the Qur'an

- *Nubuwwah and Risalah* - Belief in All Prophets of Allah, from Prophet Adam[(A.S)] to Prophet Mohammed ﷺ

- Belief in the *Day of judgment*; a day will come when every human that has ever existed will be judged by Allah about their actions in their life on earth.

- Belief in *Predestination (destiny/divine decree)* - the idea that Allah knows everything

ANGELS MENTIONED IN ISLAMIC REFERENCES

Several angels are mentioned by name in the Qur'an and Hadith, with a description of their responsibilities:

JIBRAEL (A.S) (GABRIEL)

Jibrael(A.S) is the angel in charge of communicating Allah's words to His Prophets. In Islam, the Angel Jibrael(A.S) is the transmitter of good news. He is mentioned in both the Qur'an and the Hadith. He revealed Allah's words in the form of the Qur'an to the Prophet Muhammad ﷺ. Because of this, he is also known as the Angel of Revelation. Other names for Jibrael(A.S) mentioned in Qur'an are Al-Ruh (Spirit) and, Al-Ruh-al-Ameen (Trustworthy Spirit).

"Say, ˹O Prophet,˺ "Whoever is an enemy of Jibrael should know that he revealed this ˹Quran˺ to your heart by Allah's Will, confirming what came before it—a guide and good news for the believers."
(Surah al Baqara, V:97)

The Angel Jibrael(A.S) also appeared to Bibi Maryam(A.S) (who is known as Mary in Christianity). She was the mother of Prophet Isa a.s (known as Jesus in Christianity) and considered to be the most respected woman, above all other women in the Qur'an.

"And ˹remember˺ the one who guarded her chastity, so We breathed into her through Our angel, ˹Gabriel,˺ making her and her son (Prophet Isa(a.s), a sign for all peoples."
(Surah Al-Anbya, V:91)

It is narrated in many Hadiths that Jibrael(a.s) visited the Holy Prophet(s.a.w.w) in the presence of his companions, in the form of a man in white clothes and very black hairs. It is also narrated in Hadith that The Prophet Muhammad ﷺ saw Jibrael(A.S) in his (original) form twice, and he had six hundred wings. (Sahih Muslim 174c)

MIKAEEL(A.S) (MICHAEL)

Mikaeel(A.S) is in charge of the distribution of rainfall and sustenance wherever Allah(S.W.T) wishes. He is mentioned in Qur'an once:

"Whoever is an enemy to Allah and His angels and His messengers and Jibrael and *Mikaeel*—then surely Allah is an enemy to the deniers."
(Surah al Baqara, 98)

The companions(R.A) of Allah's Apostle ﷺ have seen Mikaeel(A.S) in the human form in the battle of Uhud. It is narrated that:

Sa'ad(R.A) reported that on the Day of Uhud, I saw on the right and left side of Allah's Messenger ﷺ two persons, dressed in white clothes and whom I did not see before nor after that, and they were Jibrael and *Mikaeel* (Allah be pleased with both of them). (Sahih Muslim 2306a)

ISRAFEEL(A.S) (RAPHAEL)

After death, Muslims believe that the soul will enter Barzakh, a state of waiting until the Day of Judgement. Muslims regard life on Earth as a test from Allah(S.W.T) and their deeds will be weighed on the Day of Judgement. On this Day, the whole universe will be destroyed, and then all the beings will be resurrected for judgement by Allah(S.W.T). Israfeel(a.s) is the angel who is charged with blowing the trumpet on the Day of Judgment. The Trumpet will be blown on two different occasions, signalling the beginning of Judgment Day. The first blow will cause all creation to die, except whoever Allah spares, and the second one will cause them to be raised from the dead. Although the name Israfeel does not appear in the Qur'an, the mention is repeatedly made of an unnamed trumpet-angel assumed to identify this figure. Allah(S.W.T) revealed these events in the Qur'an as:

"And ˹beware of˺ the Day the Trumpet will be blown, and all those in the heavens and all those on the earth will be horrified ˹to the point of death˺, except those Allah wills ˹to spare˺. And all will come before Him, fully humbled."
(Surah al Naml, V:87)

"The Trumpet will be blown ˈa second timeˈ, then—behold! —they will rush from the graves to their Lord." (Surah Al-Yasin, V:51)

"On that Day all will follow the caller ˈfor assemblyˈ, ˈandˈ none will dare to deviate. All voices will be hushed before the Most Compassionate. Only whispers will be heard."
(Surah Al-Ta-ha, V:108)

"ˈAnd wait forˈ the Day ˈwhenˈ the caller will summon ˈthemˈ for something horrifying. With eyes downcast, they will come forth from the graves as if they were swarming locusts, rushing towards the caller. The disbelievers will cry, 'This is a difficult Day!'"
(Surah Al-Qamar, V:6-8)

IZRAEL[(A.S)] (AZRAEL)

Izrael[(A.S)] is the one who takes the souls with the order of Allah[(S.W.T)]. He is mentioned in the Qur'an and Hadiths as "Angel of Death."

"Say, ˈO Prophet,ˈ "Your soul will be taken by the Angel of Death, who is in charge of you. Then to your Lord, you will ˈallˈ be returned."
(Surah al Sajda, V:11)

"When death comes to any of you, Our angels take their soul, never neglecting this duty."
(Surah al An'am, V:61)

It is narrated that the Messenger of Allah ﷺ said:

'From among the people preceding your generation, there was a man whom the angel of death visited to capture his soul. (So, his soul was captured) and he was asked if he had done any good deed.' He replied, 'I don't remember any good deed.' He was asked to think it over. He said, 'I do not remember, except that I used to trade with the people in the world and I used to give a respite to the rich and forgive the poor (among my debtors). So, Allah made him enter Paradise." (Sahih Bukhari Hadith No. 3451)

KIRAMAN KATIBIN

These are the angels appointed by Allah(S.W.T), who are recording everyone's good and bad deeds. Raqeeb is the angel who sits on the right shoulder to record good deeds, and Atid is the angel who sits on the left shoulder to record evil deeds.

"As the two recording-angels—'one' sitting to the right, and 'the other to' the left—note 'everything', not a word does a person utter without having a 'vigilant' observer ready 'to write it down'."
(Surah Qaf, V:17-18)

"But no! In fact, you deny the 'final' Judgment, while you are certainly observed by vigilant, honourable angels, recording 'everything'. They know whatever you do."
(Surah Al-Infitar, V:9-12)

"He reigns supreme over all of His creation, and sends recording-angels, watching over you."
(Surah Al-An'am, V:61)

They record every detail from the life of the person to whom Allah(S.W.T) has assigned them; every thought and feeling in the person's mind, every word the person communicates, and every action that the person does. On the Day of Judgement, Kiraman Katibin will present the history records of the person to Allah. Whether Allah sends a person to Heaven or Hell for eternity will then depend on what would records show; what they thought, communicated, and did during their earthly lives. Indeed, Allah(S.W.T) is the most merciful.

MUNKAR & NAKEER

After death, two angels will question souls in the grave about their faith and deeds. Abu Huraira(R.A) reported Allah's Messenger ﷺ as saying,

"When the dead is buried, two black and blue angels, one called al-Munkar and the other an-Nakeer, come to him and ask him what opinion he held about this man (The Prophet Muhammad s.a.w.w). If he is a believer, he replies, 'He is the servant and Messenger of Allah. I testify that there is no god but Allah and that Muhammad ﷺ is His servant and apostle.' They say that they knew he would say so. A space of 4900 square cubits (a cubit is a distance between the elbow and the tip of the middle finger) is then made for him in his grave, it is illuminated for him, and he is told to sleep. He will then express a desire to return to his family to tell them but will be told to sleep like one newly married who is awakened only by the member of his family who is dearest to him until Allah resurrects him from that resting-place of his. (Mishkat al-Masabih 130)

MALIK & RIDWAN

Malik is an angel who is the gatekeeper of Hell. It is narrated in Hadith that the Holy Prophet ﷺ saw him on the night of the Mai'raj (the journey of the Prophet(A.S) from Makkah to the skies). Similarly, Ridwan is the angel who serves as the guardian of Heaven.

"O believers! Protect yourselves and your families from a Fire whose fuel is people and stones, overseen by formidable and severe angels, who never disobey whatever Allah orders—always doing as commanded." (Surah Tahrim, V:6)

HAFAZA (THE GUARDIAN ANGELS)

These angels protect human from the harm of evil jinn or shayateen. Each person is assigned four Hafaza angels, two of which keep watch during the day and two during the night.

"For each one there are successive angels before and behind, protecting them by Allah's command." (Surah Ar-Ra'd, V:10)

Allah(S.W.T) may send guardian angels to protect people from any kind of harm: physical, mental, emotional, or spiritual. So, by reciting this verse from the Qur'an, Muslims remind themselves that they are under the protective care of powerful angels who may, according to God's will, guard them against physical harm like illnesses or injuries, mental and emotional harm such as anxiety and depression, and spiritual harm that can result from the presence of evil in their lives.

Ibn Mas'ud(R.A) reported God's Messenger ﷺ as saying, "There is none of you who does not have his partner from among the jinn and his partner from among the angels put in charge of him." The hearers asked, "Does this also apply to you, Messenger of God?" He replied, "It applies to me too, but God has helped me against him, and he has accepted Islam, so he commands me to do only what is good." (Mishkat al-Masabih 67)

A man said to 'Ali ibn Abi Talib(A.S): "A group from (the tribe of) Murad wanted to kill you." Ali(A.S) said, "With every man, there are two angels who protect him from everything that is not decreed; when the decree comes, they withdraw and do not stand between him and it. A man's decreed lifespan is his protection."

HAMALAT AL-ARSH

They are the angels carrying the Arsh (Throne) of Allah(S.W.T) as mentioned in the Qur'an and Hadiths.

"The sky will then be so torn that it will be frail, with the angels on its sides. On that Day (of Judgement) eight ˹mighty angels˺ will bear the Throne of your Lord above them." (Surah Al-Haqqah, V:16-18)

These angels love believers and seek mercy and forgiveness for them.

"Those ˹angels˺ who carry the Throne and those around it glorify the praises of their Lord, have faith in Him, and seek forgiveness for the believers, ˹praying:˺ "Our Lord! You encompass everything in ˹Your˺ mercy and knowledge. So, forgive those who repent and follow Your Way, and protect them from the torment of the Hellfire. Our Lord! Admit them into the Gardens of Eternity which You have promised them, along with the righteous among their parents, spouses, and descendants. You ˹alone˺ are truly the Almighty, All-Wise. And protect them from ˹the consequences of their˺ evil deeds. For whoever You protect from the evil of their deeds on that Day will have been shown Your mercy. That is ˹truly˺ the ultimate triumph." (Surah Ghafir, V:7-9)

The Prophet ﷺ described the immensity of one of these angels in a Hadith, saying,

"I have been permitted to tell about one of Allah's angels who bears the throne; that the distance between the lobe of his ear and his shoulder is a journey of seven hundred years." (Sunan Abi Dawud)

FACTS TO REMEMBER

- One would understand the greatness of Allah(S.W.T), His power and ability, and His All-Encompassing Knowledge, from the greatness of His creation, which is a proof confirming the greatness of the Creator.

- Angels are created for the sole purpose of serving Allah(S.W.T) and made from "Noor (light)". They belong to a level of existence beyond the perceptible world of phenomena, called "Alam al-ghayb (the hidden world)". They can assume almost any form, which will appear real to the human eye.

- The Qur'an does mention that angels have wings, but Muslims don't speculate on what exactly they look like. We find it improper, for example, to make images of angels as cherubs sitting in clouds.

- When a Muslim knows that there are Angels who record all that he/she says and does and that everything he/she does is either for him/her or held against him/her, he/she would be keen to perform righteous deeds and abstain from sins, whether he/she is alone or in public.

- One would safeguard himself/herself from believing in superstitions and fables.

- One would recognise the mercy Allah(S.W.T) shows to His slaves; for Allah has assigned angels to every individual who guard him\her from evil and take care of his affairs.

JINN

- **Nature & Origin**

- **Appearance & Residence**

- **Their Special Food**

- **Human-Jinn Interactions Mentioned in the Qur'an & Hadees**

- **Iblees / Satan & Evil Jinn**

- **Intension & Trap of Satan**

- **Common Deceptions of Satan**

- **Proptecting Ourselves from the Deceptions of Satan**

NATURE & ORIGIN

Jinn is an Arabic collective noun; whose primary meaning is "to hide" or "to adapt". Some authors interpret the word to mean, literally, "beings that are concealed from the senses". Like angels, jinn are also invisible beings, and generally, humans do not have the powers to see them; thus, they are invisible to the naked eye. These supernatural creations can be seen only by Prophets and pure slaves of Allah(S.W.T). But Angels never disobey Allah; they don't have free will. However, Jinn live on the earth like human beings. There are believers and unbelievers among them. Since they have free will, they are held accountable like human beings for good and bad deeds.

Allah(S.W.T) says in the Qur'an,

"And I did not create jinn and humans except to worship Me." (Surah Al-Dhariyat, V:56)

The creation of the jinn is mentioned in the Qur'an in the following verses, Allah(S.W.T) says,

"Indeed, We created man from sounding clay moulded from black mud. As for the jinn, We created them earlier from smokeless fire." (Surah Al-Hijr, V:26-27)

The Holy Prophet ﷺ also said: "Angels were created from light and jinn from smokeless fire. And Adam(A.S) was born as he has been defined (in the Qur'an) for you (i. e. he is fashioned out of clay)." (Sahih Muslim; 2996)

Prior to the creation of Prophet Adam(A.S), Jinns were the first creation dwelled on planet Earth but led to blood-shedding and clashes. Abdullah Ibn Umar(R.A) states the following:

"Jinn, who were called Sons of Jaann, were in the world two thousand years before the creation of Prophet Adam(A.S). Allah sent an army consisting of angels against them because they caused mischief and chaos in the world, shed blood and committed murders. These mischief-makers, who were punished by angels, saved their lives by taking refuge on the islands in the sea."

APPEARANCE & RESIDENCE

The lives of jinn are very similar to humans; they eat, drink, marry, and have families. They are created in a form that can take various shapes.

The Messenger of Allah ﷺ said: "The Jinn are of three types: a type that has wings, and they fly through the air; a type that looks like snakes and dogs; and a type that stops for a rest then resumes its journey." (Al-Tabaraani in al-Kabeer, 22/214)

As mentioned in this hadith, we came to know that some jinn have wings and can fly through the air, some are creeping, such as snake or scorpion, and some do not have permanent residence and continuously moving from one place to another. Muslim scholars described that the places commonly used by the jinn to stay are: the villages, mountains and the bay. And the usual sites visited by them, and sometimes used as a residence, are toilet, ocean, market, roofs, landfills and graves. Apart from these places, they also like quiet areas, such as valleys, deserts, and rocky mountains.

The Messenger of Allah ﷺ said: These privies are frequented by the jinns and devils. So, when anyone amongst you goes there, he should say: "I seek refuge in Allah from male and female devils." (Sunan Abi Dawud 6)

THEIR SPECIAL FOOD

The jinn and their animal kingdom have unique foods, and the remains of the food of human beings are eatable to them. A conversation between the Holy Prophet ﷺ and some jinn gives us an idea about this,

A deputation of the jinn came to the Prophet ﷺ and said: "O Prophet Muhammad ﷺ, forbid your community to cleanse themselves with a bone or dung or charcoal, for in them Allah (S.W.T) has provided sustenance for us." So, the Prophet ﷺ forbade people to do so. (Sunan Abi Dawud 39)

"They (the Jinn) asked him (the Holy Prophet s.a.w.w) about their provision, and he said: 'Every bone on which the name of Allah is recited is your provision. The time it will fall in your hand, it would be covered with flesh, and the dung of (the camels) is fodder for your animals.' The Messenger of Allah ﷺ said (to the companions): 'Don't perform istinja (cleanse) with these (things), for these are the food of your brothers (Jinn).' (Sahih Muslim 450a)

HUMAN-JINN INTERACTIONS MENTIONED IN THE QUR'AN AND HADITH

Since the existence of jinn is definite by the Qur'an and Hadith, denying them will damage the Islamic faith. Jinn are mentioned several times in the Qur'an; in fact, there is a whole chapter in it, named "Al-Jinn; Chapter/Surah 72".

As revealed in the Qur'an, Jinn must also worship Allah(S.W.T) as humans do for their salvation on the Day of Judgement. Their life purpose is not very different from that of humans because Allah(S.W.T) has commanded them to do the same good works as humans and are supposed to obey and worship Allah Al-Mighty. As in humans, there are two larger categories, Muslims and non-Muslims; similarly, among Jinns there are the same two main divisions (Muslim and non-Muslim). Non-muslim jinn can also become Muslims if they take inspiration from the Islamic religion. The chain of Prophets and Messengers of Allah(S.W.T) also guided jinn towards worshipping the One and only God, Allah Al-Mighty.

THE KINGDOM OF PROPHET SULAIMAN(A.S)

Among the previous religions, the prominent interaction of Humans and Jinn described in the Qur'an is in the era of Prophet Sulaiman(A.S). Prophet Dawud(A.S) was a wise king, and when he passed away, his son, Prophet Sulaiman(A.S), became king. He pleaded Allah(S.W.T) for a kingdom so big and powerful, such as none after him would have, and Allah granted his wish. Besides wisdom, Allah had blessed Sulaiman(A.S) with many miracles. He could control the winds, and utilising this authority, he could easily travel interminable distances within a brief period. He was given the knowledge to understand and talk to birds and animals. The Jinn were also under the command of Sulaiman(A.S). He was the only person to whom Allah had granted the power to control Jinns. He could command them and utilise them for his service and even make them suffer for disobedience.

One day, Sulaiman(A.S) had gathered his army, comprising humans, animals, birds, jinn and of course, wind. The sharp eyes of Sulaiman(A.S) noticed the absence of one hoopoe bird (hud-hud) in the vast gathering. He decided to severely punish or imposing the death penalty on the bird as a non-disciplinary action, but he gave the bird a chance to explain the reason behind its absence. He sent signals all over the kingdom to call on him, but it was nowhere to be found.

Eventually, the hoopoe came to Sulaiman(A.S) and explained the reason for its delay.

"I have discovered something of which you are not aware of. I have come from Sheba (Sab'a) with important news." Sulaiman(A.S) became curious, and his anger subsided.

The bird continued: "Beyond the knowledge of Sulaiman(A.S), there is a kingdom named Sheba, which was being ruled by a Queen named 'Bilqis', who owned lots of things including a splendid Throne. But despite all this wealth, Satan has entered her heart and the hearts of her people. She rules their minds completely. It shocked me to learn that they worship the sun instead of Allah, the Almighty."

To check the hoopoe's information, Sulaiman(A.S) sent a letter to the Queen with the bird and waited for the response. He instructed the bird to remain hidden and to watch everything.

After reading his letter, she sent her high officials to the Kingdom of Prophet Sulaiman(A.S). They returned and described their Queen the massiveness of his army. Instead of taking offence, she decided to visit Prophet Sulaiman(A.S). Accompanied by her royal officials and servants, she left Sheba, sending a messenger ahead to inform Sulaiman(A.S) that she was on her way to meet him.

Sulaiman(A.S) asked the jinn in his employ whether anyone among them could bring her throne to his palace before she arrives.

One of them said, "I will bring it to you before this sitting is over."

Sulaiman(A.S) did not react to this offer; it appeared that he was waiting for a faster means. The jinn competed with each other to please him.

One of them, named 'Ifrit', said: "I will fetch it for you in the twinkling of an eye!"

No sooner had this one - who had the knowledge of the Book - finished his phrase than the throne stood before Sulaiman(A.S). The mission had, indeed, been completed in the blinking of an eye. Prophet Sulaiman(A.S) throne was in Palestine, and the throne of Bilqis had been in Yemen, two thousand miles away. This was a great miracle performed by one of those believers sitting with Prophet Sulaiman(A.S).

PROPHET MUHAMMAD ﷺ AND THE COMMUNITY OF JINN

Before the advent of Islam, evil jinn (Satan) had the power to travel and eavesdrop on any important news from the angels of the visible sky of this world. They manage to overhear and carries it to their friends. And when the Angels see the jinn, they attack them with meteors. Then they narrate what they heard, alloying it with lies and make additions to it. But after the birth of Prophet Muhammad ﷺ and the spread of Islam, jinn were unable to hear a tiny detail of news from the skies. Angels of the skies started bombarding them with meteors when they came to sneak. A companion, Ibn Abbas(R.A), narrated a hadith, describing this event and the revelation of Surah Jinn:

Allah's Messenger ﷺ went out along with a group of his companions towards `Ukaz Market. At that time, something intervened between the devils and the news of the Heaven, and flames were sent down upon them, so the devils returned. Their fellow-devils said, "What is wrong with you? " They said, "Something has intervened between us and the news of the Heaven, and fires (flames) have been shot at us." Their fellow-devils said, "Nothing has intervened between you and the news of the Heaven, but an important event has happened. Therefore, travel all over the world, east and west, and try to find out what has happened." And so they set out and travelled all over the world, east and west, looking for that thing which intervened between them and the news of the Heaven. Those of the devils who had set out towards Tihama went to Allah's Messenger (ﷺ) at Nakhla (a place between Makkah and Taif) while he was on his way to Ukaz Market. (They met him) while he was offering the Fajr prayer with his companions. When they heard the Holy Qur'an being recited (by Allah's Messenger ﷺ), they listened to it and said (to each other). This is the thing which has intervened between you and the news of the Heavens." Then they returned to their people and said, "O our people! We have really heard a wonderful recital (Qur'an). It gives guidance to the right, and we have believed therein. We shall not join in worship, anybody with our Lord." Then Allah(S.W.T) revealed to His Prophet ﷺ (i.e., Surah al-Jinn). (Bukhari 4921)

At that time, Allah(S.W.T) revealed the following verses of Surah Jinn,

"Say, ˹O Prophet,˺ "It has been revealed to me that a group of jinn listened ˹to the Qur'an,˺ and said ˹to their fellow jinn˺: 'Indeed, we have heard a wondrous recitation. It leads to Right Guidance, so we believed in it, and we will never associate anyone with our Lord ˹in worship˺.

[Surah Jinn; 1-2]

There is another Hadith which tells us about the interactions of Messenger of Allah ﷺ with the community of Jinn, and preaching Islam to them,

Ibn Masood(R.A) narrated that we were in the company of the Messenger of Allah ﷺ one night and we missed him. We searched for him in the valleys and the hills and said: "He has either been taken away (by jinn) or has been secretly killed." He (the narrator) said: "We spent the worst night which people could ever spend. When it was dawn, we saw him coming from the side of Hiri'." He (the narrator) reported: "We said:' Messenger of Allah, we missed you and searched for you, but we could not find you and we spent the worst night which people could ever spend.' He (the Holy Prophet s.a.w.w) said: "There came to me an inviter on behalf of the Jinn, and I went along with him and recited to them the Qur'an." He (the narrator) said: "He then went along with us and showed us their traces and traces of their embers. They (the Jinn) asked him (the Holy Prophet s.a.w.w) about their provision, and he said: 'Every bone on which the name of Allah is recited is your provision. The time it will fall in your hand, it would be covered with flesh, and the dung of (the camels) is fodder for your animals.' The Messenger of Allah ﷺ said: "Don't perform istinja with these (things) for these are the food of your brothers (Jinn)." (Sahih Muslim 450a)

INTERACTIONS OF JINN WITH PEOPLE OTHER THAN PROPHETS(A.S)

Mother of the Believers, Syeda Ai'sha(R.A) said: "Allah's Messenger ﷺ told his wives a story one night, and one of them said: "It sounds like a fable of Khurafa!" He said: "Do you know what that means? Khurafa was a man from [the Yemenite tribe of] Udhra. The jinn captured him in the pagan era [al-jahiliyya], so he stayed with them for a long time, then they returned him to his people. He used to tell the people about the marvels that he saw among them, so the people said: 'The fable of Khurafa.'" (Ash-Shama'il Al-Muhammadiyah, 251)

As human beings cannot see jinn, we should take protective measures according to Islam's teachings to save ourselves from the impairment of the evil ones within them.

As narrated Jabir ibn Abdullah(R.A): The Prophet ﷺ said: "Do not go out often after the night is still. Allah has animals which he sends out. Anyone who hears the barking of a dog or the braying of a donkey should seek refuge with Allah from the Accursed Shaytan. They see what you do not see." (Al-Adab Al-Mufrad)

AbuSa'id al-Khudri(R.A) narrated: The Messenger of Allah ﷺ said: "Some snakes are jinn; so when anyone sees one of them in his house, he should give it a warning three times. If it returns (after that), he should kill it, for it is a devil. (Sunan Abi Dawud, 5256)

IBLESS / SATAN AND EVIL JINN

When Allah(S.W.T) decided to create human beings, a being who will surpass all ranks in knowledge than the previous other creatures, He asked his angels to collect clay from the Earth. The obedient Angels collected clay, and Allah(S.W.T) made a man-like figure with it and named him Adam(A.S). But the figure didn't move for forty long years. It just stood still there. When Iblees, a jinn, who was like a teacher of the Angels at that time, saw this figure, he was confused and scared.

After forty years, Allah(S.W.T) breathed spirit into Adam(A.S). He gave Adam(A.S) vast knowledge of the things present in the entire universe. Then He asked all the Angels, including Iblees, to prostrate before Adam(A.S) as a sign of respect. One by one, all the Angels prostrated before the Prophet except Iblees. Prostration, in this context, does not mean worship but for an act of respect. It was allowed to prostrate in respect for the humans in some previous religions; a similar occurrence can be found in Surah Yusuf(A.S), where Prophet Yaqoob(A.S), his wife, and his eleven children knelt before Prophet Yusuf(A. S).

"And ʿrememberʾ when We said to the angels, "Prostrate before Adam," so they all did—but not Iblîs, who was one of the jinn, but he rebelled against the command of his Lord." (Surah Kahf, V:50)

Iblees said that he was better and superior to the Prophet, and he was made from fire. He didn't understand the will of Allah and refused to obey Allah's command. Allah(S.W.T) got angry with this disobedience. So, he banished Iblees from paradise. He was now an outcast. From that day, Iblees was called 'the Satan/Shaitaan ' and will be thrown into Hell on the Day of Judgement. Shaitaan was now furious with the humans as he was banished from the paradise because of them. He vowed to take revenge by misleading the humans in the way of Allah. Allah(S.W.T) gave him the time period till the Day of Judgement and told that he cannot misled a true servant of Allah. This whole conservation is described in Qur'an very clearly;

Allah asked, "O Iblis! What is the matter with you that you did not join others in prostration?"
He replied, "It is not for me to prostrate to a human You created from sounding clay moulded from black mud."
Allah commanded, "Then get out of Paradise, for you are truly cursed.
And surely upon you is condemnation until the Day of Judgment."
Satan appealed, "My Lord! Then delay my end until the Day of their resurrection."

Allah said, "You will be delayed until the appointed Day."
Satan responded, "My Lord! For allowing me to stray I will surely tempt them on earth and mislead them all together, except Your chosen servants among them."
Allah said, 'This path leads to me straight. You will certainly have no authority over My servants, except the deviant who follows you, and surely Hell is their destined place, all together. It has seven gates, to each a group of them is designated."
Indeed, the righteous will be amid Gardens and springs.
(Surah Al-Hijr, 32-45)

INTENTION & TRAP OF SATAN MENTIONED IN QUR'AN & HADITH

"He (Satan) said, "For leaving me to stray I will lie in ambush for them on Your Straight Path. I will approach them from their front, their back, their right, their left, and then You will find most of them ungrateful." (Surah Al-A'raf, 16-17)

"O humanity! Indeed, Allah's promise is true. So do not let the life of this world deceive you, nor let the chief deceiver (Satan) deceive you about Allah. Surely Satan is an enemy to you, so take him as an enemy. He only invites his followers to become inmates of the Blaze." (Surah Fatir, 5-6)

As the verses of the Qur'an warns us about the evil designs of Satan and his followers, we should recognise this threat and advance towards the guidance given by the Allah Al-Mighty and the Messenger of Allah ﷺ to save our Islamic believes.

Abu Dharr[(R.A)] narrated:

"I entered the Masjid, and the Messenger of Allah [s.a.w.w] was there, so I came and sat before him, and he said: 'O Abu Dharr, seek refuge with Allah from the evils of the devils among the Jinn and mankind.' I said: 'Are there devils among mankind?' He said: 'Yes.'" (Sunan an-Nasa'I, 5507)

Jinn have the power to see us, but we (humans) cannot see them. The nonbelievers among the jinn, the followers or soldiers of Satan, try to lead us astray and try to lead us away from the remembrance of Allah[(S.W.T)].

Allah(S.W.T) has already told us about this in Sura Al-Araf, verse 27:

"O children of Adam! Do not let Satan deceive you as he tempted your parents out of Paradise and caused their cover to be removed to show them their private parts. Surely, he and his soldiers watch you from where you cannot see them. We have made the devils allies of those who disbelieve."
(Sura Al-Araf, verse 27)

The above verse makes it clear that jinn have the power to see humans and take possession of humans. The only way to protect ourselves from evil beings is to walk in the path that Allah and His Messenger ﷺ have shown us and follow the teachings of the Qur'an, Sunnah and Hadith.

COMMON DECEPTIONS OF SATAN

Disbelief in the Oneness of God:

The foundation of Islam is the belief in the Tawhid; Oneness of Allah - having no partner, equal, son or rivals. Conversely, the greatest sin is to ascribe partners or equals with Allah, for e.g Directing worship to other than Allah, Delegating Allah's attributes to other objects or beings (e.g. idols/lucky charms), Claiming that Allah has a son, mother or any other partner etc. Thus, tempting mankind into Shirk is Satan's primary focus. Such beliefs contradict the fact that Allah alone has power and knowledge over all things and is the Only One Who can bring benefit or harm.

Innovation in the Religion:

Satan will lure a person to invent wrong beliefs and practices into Islam which were neither ordained by Allah(S.W.T) nor the Prophet Muhammad ﷺ. This is a great danger to a Muslim's faith, as the people who follow innovations believe their acts are accepted, although, in reality, they are committing a sin. These innovators will feel no need for repentance, as they do not recognise their wrongdoing.

Gradual Deception Of Neglecting Obligatory Deeds:

Allah(S.W.T) has made certain actions obligatory on every Muslim, the most regular of which is the five daily prayers, i.e., the Salah. Satan seeks to make us neglectful of prayers and other good deeds, driving us away from the remembrance of Allah and his Prophet ﷺ.

"Satan's plan is to stir up hostility and hatred between you with intoxicants and gambling, and to prevent you from remembering Allah and praying. Will you not then refrain?" (Surah Al-Ma'idah, V:91)

The gradual deception is used in many ways. For example, Satan tricks people into desiring to cease their obligatory religious acts. Initially, convincing people to give up their optional acts of worship, which leads them to become lazy with the obligatory ones. He also tries to trivialise small sins, leading them down a slippery slope to major sins.

Beautifying Evil Deeds & Arousing Desires:

"and Satan made their misdeeds appealing to them." (Surah An'am, 43)

Satan tricks people into forbidden acts instead of those which are permitted by presenting sins in an attractive way, such as music over the Qur'an, haram income over halal, and into the small percentage of prohibited food and drink over the vast majority that is wholesome and pure.

Satan plays on human's desires and temptations, and convinces them to indulge in instant gratification without considering the consequences. This inevitably leads to regret and humiliation, either in this life or on the Day of Judgement.

"And whoever takes Satan as a guardian instead of Allah, has certainly suffered a tremendous loss. Satan only makes them ˋfalseˋ promises and deludes them with ˋemptyˋ hopes. Truly Satan promises them nothing but delusion." (Surah An-Nisa, V:119-120)

Overlooking The Rights Of The People Around Us:

There are rights on every muslim that they owe to other believers and humanity, and there are rights of every soul on another. Satan also made us often overlook the importance of these rights and tricks us to feel that since we are saying our prayers etc. regularly, therefore all will remain well for us; neglecting the duty to be kind to our parents, help our neighbours, poor and orphans, visiting the sick, not to hurt anyone by our words or actions etc.

Once Prophet Muhammad ﷺ was asked, "O Messenger of Allah! A certain woman prays in the night, fasts in the day, does pious actions and gives charity, but she injures and hurt her neighbours with her tongue." The Messenger of Allah ﷺ said, "There is no good in her. She will go to Fire." The Sahaba said, "Another woman prays only the prescribed prayers and gives very little as charity and does not injure anyone. Her neighbours are happy with her attitude." The Messenger of Allah ﷺ said, "She is one of the people of Paradise." [Bukhari in Al-Adabul Mufrad]

May Allah(S.W.T) guide us to understand the importance of Haqooq-ul Ibaad (the rights of the people) so that we may discharge the duties with the same fervour as we try to fulfil Haqooq Allah (the rights of Allah) (Aameen).

PROTECTING OURSELVES FROM THE DECEPTION OF THE SATAN

Seeking Refuge Of Allah(S.W.T):

We must ask Allah for His protection and rely on Him alone for help and protection from Satan. Surah Al-Falaq and An-Nas of the Qu'ran may be recited regularly. We must realise that Satan will never give up attempting to mislead us as long as we are alive. We must always be on our guard and constantly ask Allah for guidance and protection.

"If you are tempted by Satan, then seek refuge with Allah. Surely, He is All-Hearing, All-Knowing. Indeed, when Satan whispers to those mindful ˹of Allah˺, they remember ˹their Lord˺ then they start to see ˹things˺ clearly." (Surah Al-A'raf, V:200-201)

It is narrated that The Messenger of Allah ﷺ used to seek refuge from the evil eye of the jinn and mankind. When the Verses of Refuge (Surah Al-Falaq & An-Nas) were revealed, he started to recite them and stopped reciting anything else." (Sunan Ibn Majah, Book 31, Hadith 76)

Seek Forgiveness:

If we succumb to Satan's plots, by the Grace and Mercy of Allah(S.W.T) we still have the opportunity to rectify our mistakes by acknowledging our wrongdoings and repenting to Allah.

The Prophet (peace be upon him) said, "Satan said to the Lord of Glory, 'By Your Glory O Lord, I will keep trying to misguide Your slaves so long as their souls are in their bodies.' The Lord said, 'By My Glory and Majesty, I will continue to forgive them so long as they ask My forgiveness.'" (Ahmad)

For repentance to be accepted, it must be sincere, with the intention of never committing that same sin again. The Holy Prophet ﷺ said, "He who repents from sin is like the one without sin." (Ibn Majah)

Avoid Sinful Environments & Keep Good Companionship:

The company you keep strongly influences your decisions and actions. Good companions will remind you about Allah and encourage you to do good, whereas a bad company will lead you into the arms of Satan. We must, therefore, distance ourselves from anything that may lead to sinning.

"Be gracious, enjoin what is right, and turn away from those who act ignorantly." (Surah Al-A'raf, V:199)

The Messenger of Allah ﷺ advised, "A person is on the path of his close friend, so be careful whom you befriend." (Tirmidhi)

Keep Doing Good Deeds And Be Humble To Allah:

By increasing the frequency of our good deeds and keeping us busy with gaining knowledge of the Qur'an and Hadith, it is excellent protection from Satan. If one occupies their time with good the whole day, they are less likely to be influenced by Satan's tricks. We should always remember that Satan was an outcast due to his arrogance, so no matter how pious we become, we should always be humble to Allah Al-Mighty and keep in mind that all our deeds are acceptable only by the will of Allah(S.W.T).

On the Day of Judgement, Satan will confess to his sins and mischief. He will declare before all of creation that Allah(S.W.T) is the One who tells the truth and that he (Satan) is a liar.

We ask Allah the Almighty, by His most beautiful Names and sublime Attributes, to forgive our sins and grant us refuge from the traps of Satan.

AMEEN

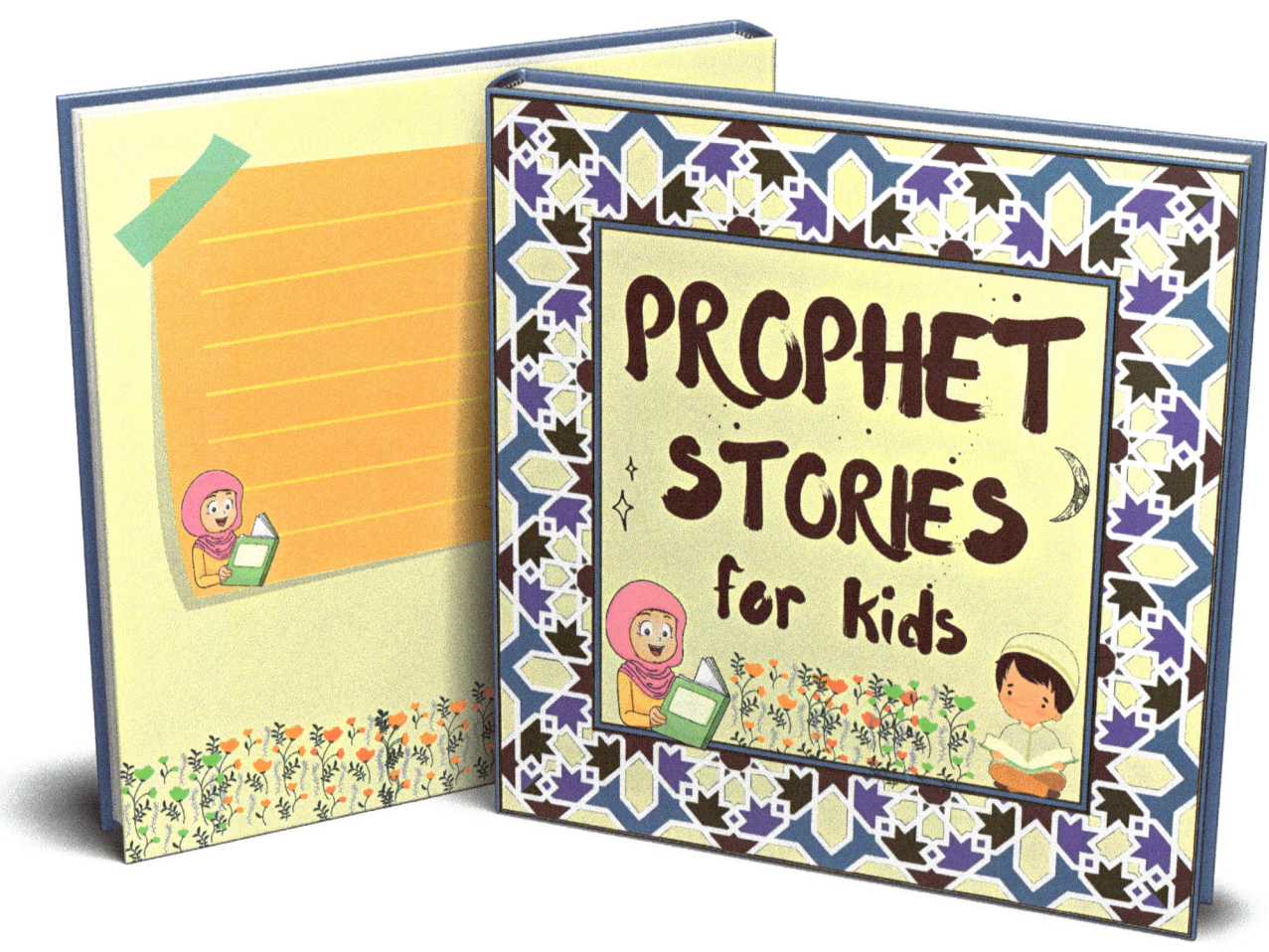

ISBN 978-1-990544-43-9

*Search ISBN on the retailer website

Premium Color Pages Hardcover

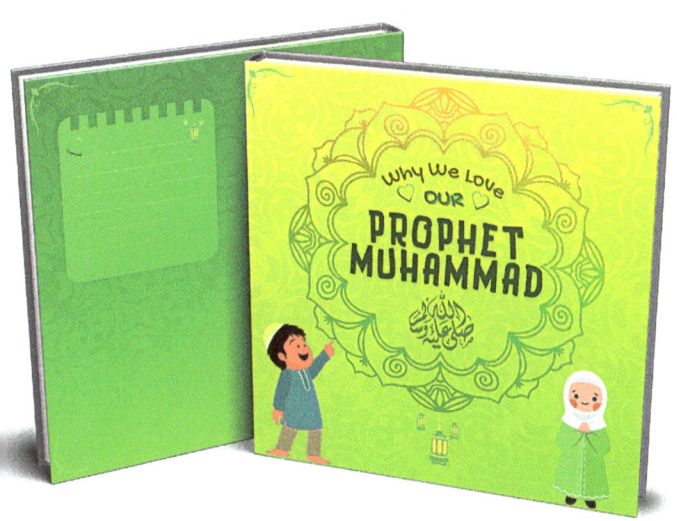

ISBN 978-1-990544-42-2

ISBN 978-1-990544-41-5

ISBN 978-1-990544-45-3

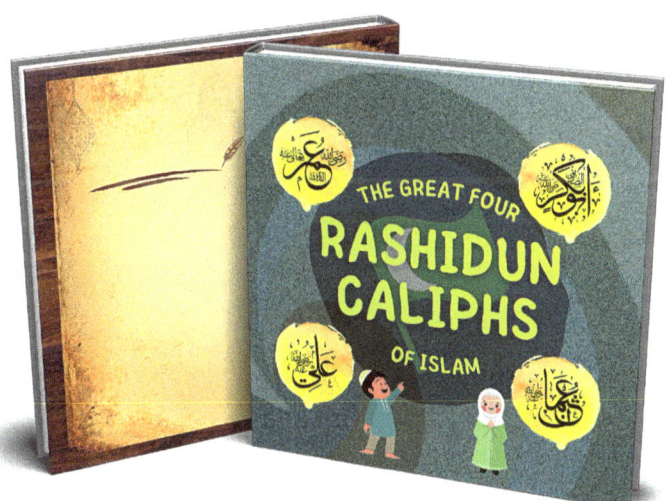

ISBN 978-1-990544-44-6

*Search ISBN on the retailer website